Rebecca

Contents

Acknowledgements
Thanks to Allan Skipp for compiling the text.
The publishers would like to thank Leon Paul Equipment Co Ltd for their contribution to this book.

 **Paul**

Leon Paul Equipment Co Ltd, 14 New North Street, London WC1N 3PW.

Photography by Karina Hoskyns.
Illustrations by Taurus Graphics.

1

Foreword

The modern sport of fencing has been included in every Olympic Games since Baron de Coubertin revived the ancient games in 1896.

At the highest level, fencing is physically demanding, requiring intense concentration and tactical awareness. However, many fencers who never aspire to Olympic heights regularly attend clubs and compete at regional and national levels.

Some find fencing an excellent way of maintaining general fitness without the risk of injury. The sport suits men, women and children of all ages, and is one of the few physical activities in which males and females take part on equal terms.

Fencing often appeals to those who are reluctant to take part in team games. They enjoy the individuality of the sport, matching their own skill, speed and intellect against those of an opponent. Others enjoy the aesthetic pleasure of perfecting and performing disciplined movements correctly, and studying the theory and language of fencing for achievement awards.

Fencing for participants in wheelchairs is a major sport in competitions for those with disabilities. Certain disabilities prove to be of little disadvantage when fencing, and those who are unable to compete at other sports find that they can compete on equal terms with able-bodied fencers.

The Amateur Fencing Association (AFA) is the national governing body in the UK, organising an ongoing development programme which includes the training of new coaches and supporting clubs and fencers.

There is a nationally-organised series of championships at foil, épée and sabre for men, women and teams, and several international events.

There are fencing clubs in most areas, regularly organising classes for new fencers and having equipment for loan.

Individual membership of the AFA is open to all new fencers, regardless of standard, and members regularly receive information on fencing events, *The Sword* magazine, notices and reports of competitions, local organisers and clubs, etc.

For more details, write to: General Secretary, Amateur Fencing Association, 1 Barons Gate, 33–35 Rothschild Road, London W4 5HT.

Note Throughout the book fencers are referred to individually as 'he'. This should, of course, to taken to mean 'he or she' where appropriate. All measurements are given in metric units.

Introduction

The sword is one of the oldest of weapons, and there have been many types used by armies through the centuries. Most had heavy, broad blades, and required strong arms to hack through adversaries, either on foot or on horseback.

As the use of armour developed as a means of protection, so swords became larger and heavier, until two hands were required to wield the mighty weapons.

With the invention of gunpowder, the musket and bayonet replaced the sword for military use, though small swords were carried for personal protection.

The duelling rapier evolved with a long-tapering blade which culminated in a sharp point, and was used to settle 'matters of honour' and to test a gentleman's swordsmanship. To achieve proficient use of the sword, a gentleman would take lessons from a fencing master.

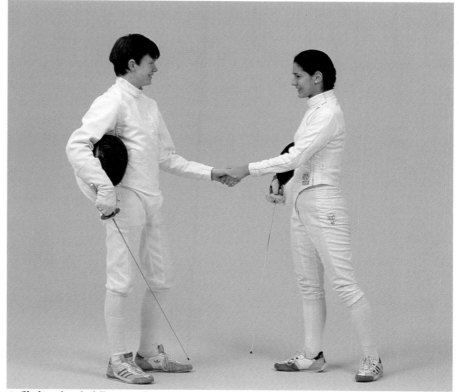

▲ *Shaking hands following a bout*

Many of the rules and conventions governing fencing – the tradition of saluting before a bout and the shaking of hands at the end – still reflect the sport's aristocratic origins.

▼ *The salute before crossing swords*

The salute

Fencing has always been and always will be a chivalrous sport, so it is customary to salute your opponent before a bout or competition. It is also a courtesy to salute your coach before and after receiving a lesson.

With your mask under one arm and your sword in the other hand, place your feet, heels touching, at right angles, your sword pointing downwards to the front. Raise the sword arm straight, bring it back to a perpendicular position, guard in line with the lips, then sweep it away, point downwards, to the original starting position.

Weapons

Three types of sword are used. There are left- and right-handed versions, and smaller sizes are available for children.

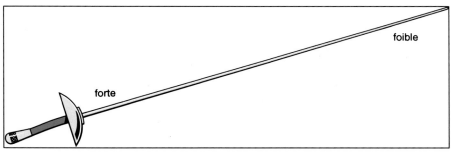

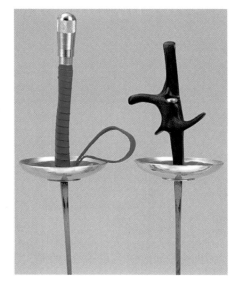

▲ *The foil – a light, flexible weapon, weighing 500 g. Thrusts with the point at the opponent's trunk count as valid hits. The blade is rectangular or square in section, and must not be more than 90 cm in length. The overall length of the weapon must not exceed 110 cm. The point must be flattened and covered with a rubber or plastic button or, in the case of an electric foil, a sprung metal point assembly. The circular guard must pass through a gauge of 12 cm diameter.*

Different types of handle are commonly used. These may be 'French', or straight, handles which are usually covered with leather or rubber, or moulded 'orthopaedic', or 'pistol' grip, handles, which have finger protrusions.

French handle foils have pommels which act as a counter balance to the blade. A leather loop, known as a 'martingale', is fitted between the guard pad and the handle. It is held in the fingers of the sword hand and ensures that the foil is not wrenched from the fencer's hand during a bout.

Orthopaedic handles have many designs and may be moulded in plastic or aluminium. But they may not have attachments which aid in the protection of the user, or have protrusions which extend beyond the guard, or be designed in such a way as to allow the opponent's blade to become entangled in them, or exceed the overall maximum length of the weapon. Orthopaedic foils do not normally need a martingale

◄ *Foil: 'French' grip (left) and 'orthopaedic' or 'pistol' grip (right)*

The épée – a development of the duelling ▶ rapier and heavier than the foil, weighing 770 g. Valid hits are scored by thrusting the point at any part of the opponent's body, arms, legs and head. The blade has a triangular section and is the same length and is grooved as the foil. It must have a protected point or sprung metal point assembly. The guard must have a maximum diameter of 13.5 cm, and helps to protect the épée fencer's forearm. The rules governing handles are the same as those for the foil

forte

foible

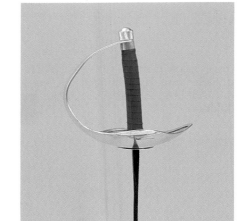

▲ *The sabre*

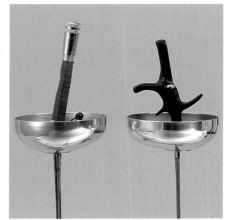

▲ *Epée: 'French grip' (left) and 'orthopaedic' or 'pistol' grip (right)*

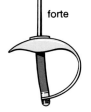

foible

forte

◀ *The sabre – a lighter, more flexible version of the military sabre. Hits are scored by using edge 'cuts' or point thrusts. Hits scored on the opponent's body above the hips, arms and head count as valid. The sabre is the same weight as the foil, 500 g. The total length must not exceed 105 cm. The blade is approximately rectangular in section. The guard is shaped to protect the sword hand and forearm, and it must pass through a gauge 15 cm × 14 cm*

Weapon parts

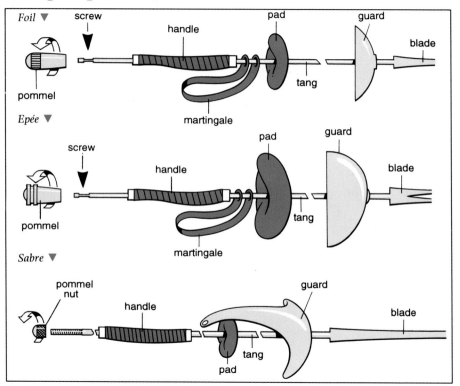

Foil ▼

screw

pommel

handle

pad

martingale

tang

guard

blade

Epée ▼

screw

pommel

handle

pad

martingale

tang

guard

blade

Sabre ▼

pommel nut

handle

pad

tang

guard

blade

Clothing

Protective clothing for fencing is made to the highest standard and is designed to look good and be practical.

The rules lay down that the fencer must be dressed in white from head to foot, and the jacket must overlap the breeches by at least 10 cm at the waist.

An 'under-plastron' should be worn under the jacket. This provides extra protection under the sword arm and part of the chest and back.

Breeches must fasten under the knee, and long socks must cover the legs.

Jackets for women have pockets for chest protectors, and these should always be used.

One glove is worn on the sword hand and this has a long cuff to cover the jacket sleeve at least halfway between the wrist and the elbow.

▲ Man, woman and child in full kit, holding mask

▲ Under-plastron worn under the fencing jacket to provide extra protection under the arm

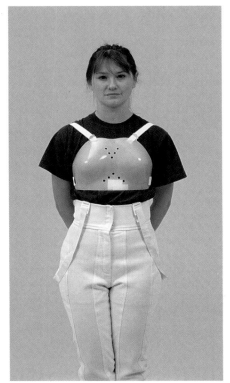

▲ *Full chest protectors*

▲ *Individual chest protectors*

▲ *Masks must be adjusted to fit snugly*

9

Basic movements

The On Guard

This is the 'get ready' position for fencing and enables the fencer to be balanced and constantly ready to change direction while continuing to threaten the opponent with the weapon.

Start by standing with your feet about hip width apart, body upright and weight equally distributed on both feet. Let your arms hang by your sides.

Bend both knees, keeping the body upright and your weight evenly on both feet. If you are right-handed, keep your left foot still and pivot your right foot – the leading foot – round on the heel until it is at right angles to your left foot. If you are left-handed, pivot your left foot.

Your knees should point in the same direction as your feet, with your body upright. Your heels should still be in line and you should be looking in the direction of your leading foot. Lift your sword arm so it is directly over your leading leg, with the hand at about breast height. Bend your elbow until it is about the distance of your own hand span from your body.

Your non-sword arm should be raised in a bent arm position just away from your body, with the wrist bent and the hand relaxed at about shoulder height.

This is the 'On Guard' for foil and épée. For sabre the sword hand is much lower, usually below waist height, and the non-sword arm is held low and well back to avoid being hit.

Practise coming 'On Guard' in one movement, preferably in front of a mirror, looking straight ahead.

It is very important that you can relax your shoulders and arms in the correct position with the body upright. You must practise until you feel comfortable in coming 'On Guard' instinctively.

◀ *Two fencers on a piste*

For right-handers, ▶ *keep the left foot still and pivot the right foot round on the heel until it is at right angles to the left*

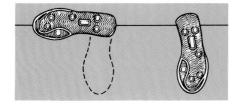

▲ ▲ *Right-handed On Guard (from front and side)*

▼ ▼ *Left-handed On Guard (from front and side)*

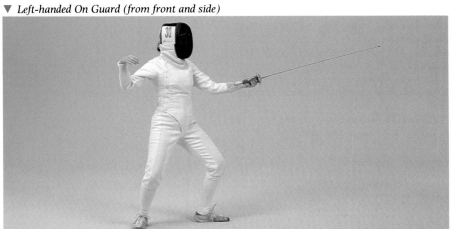

Moving forwards and backwards

When stepping forwards, both feet move one step, unlike walking. The front foot is moved forwards just clearing the ground, with the heel contacting the ground first while the rear foot, keeping equal distance, moves forwards with the toe contacting the ground first. The balance is maintained by keeping the weight between the feet and moving from the knee and not the hip. The heels are kept in line with each other and the knees above the insteps.

When stepping backwards, the reverse is the case. The rear foot, just clearing the ground, is moved backwards with the toe contacting the ground first while the front foot, keeping equal distance, moves backwards with the heel contacting the ground first.

Although these are the mechanical actions, while keeping the basic principles in mind, it is best not to dwell too much on them because a stiff, jerky action will result. Remember not to close the feet together.

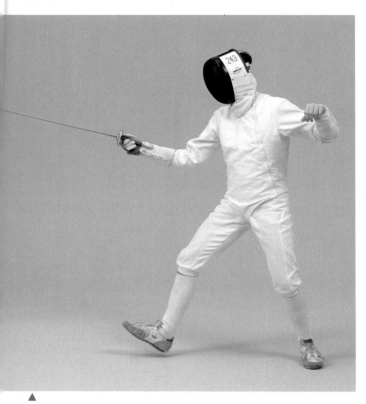

▲   ▲

◀ *Steps forwards begin by moving the leading foot. After each step the fencer must be 'On Guard'*

Lunge and recovery

When lunging, your sword must cover the distance from wherever you are to the opponent's target as quickly as possible, with the minimal exposure of your own target.

First straighten the arm slowly and smoothly. Try to make the effort come from the elbow, and do not punch from the shoulder. The hand should finish in line with the shoulder, palm uppermost. Now step forwards while straightening the arm, and practise this a few times.

As the arm is straightening, clear the front foot from the ground toe first (almost the same action as the step forwards) while pushing from the back foot, straightening the back leg as you do so and allowing the back arm to drop and the hand, palm uppermost, to rest lightly on the back thigh. Study the photographs to the right carefully.

Lunge and recovery. The sword arm must ▶ *begin straightening first. Then kick forwards with the front foot and push with the rear leg until the latter is straight. Recovery to the On Guard begins by bending the rear leg*

①

②

14

③

These are the points to check when you are on the lunge:

- your back foot should be flat on the ground
- back knee straight
- sword arm straight and shoulder high
- back arm down
- head and body upright.

You must practise this as much as possible, each time increasing the drive as the back leg is straightened, thus making each lunge faster.

The lunge and recovery are usually executed as one movement. As the heel hits the ground, use the rebound action to carry the front foot backwards, simultaneously bending the back knee and lifting the back arm (the back arm aids a balanced and efficient recovery). When the front heel touches the ground, bend the sword arm.

Now you should be back in the On Guard position, perfectly balanced, ready to move backwards or forwards or to attack again.

④

Flèche

The flèche is another way of reaching the target, but is a much more tactical offensive action and must be done at the right time and distance.

'Flèche' is the French word for arrow, and this describes the movement; the point leads and the rest of the body follows as near horizontally as possible.

As you straighten your arm, shift the centre of gravity forwards, rapidly tipping your body towards the horizontal, trying to keep the front knee bent for as long as possible. As your back foot leaves the ground and starts to swing past the front foot, push off from the latter, propelling yourself quickly and powerfully forwards, both feet leaving the ground for a fraction of a second, the body near horizontal.

The hit must arrive on the target before the back foot touches the ground.

▲   ▲
◀ *Flèche. The sword arm must begin straightening. Then drive forwards with a loss of balance*

17

Balestra

The balestra is a short, sharp jump forwards, used to surprise the opponent before making an attack, or used to draw the opponent's attack.

The action is similar to a step forwards, but as you lift your front foot, jump forwards sharply from the rear foot and land both feet simultaneously.

Balestra. A short, sharp jump forwards ▶ ▼

Fencing with the foil

When fencing with the foil, valid hits are scored by thrusting the foil point at the opponent's trunk. Hits on the arms, legs or head do not count as valid and are considered 'off target'.

A valid hit must be made with sufficient force to slightly bend the foil blade such that if the point had been sharp, it would have pierced the flesh.

During a bout either fencer may choose to attack, and the attack is defined in the rules as: *an offensive action made by a fencer who is extending his sword arm and is directing his foil point towards the opponent's trunk.*

Therefore, an attack may be considered to be a reaching forwards to hit one's opponent on the body with the foil point.

If, during a bout, one fencer chooses to attack his opponent, then the opponent must recognise this as a valid attempt to score a hit, and must try to defend himself by deflecting the oncoming point with his own foil.

However, if at this moment the opponent is surprised by the attack and reacts by hitting back without first deflecting the oncoming point, then the attacking fencer will be awarded the hit even if they both hit simultaneously, provided the attack hits on the valid target.

If the defender is successful in deflecting the attacking blade, then he may immediately hit back, and the attacker must try to defend.

The exchange of alternatively hitting and defending occurs each time either fencer chooses to attack, and continues until one fencer makes a hit, either valid or off target, or until the exchange is broken off.

If both fencers choose exactly the same moment to attack by simultaneously extending their sword arms, and both succeed in hitting each other, then neither will score the hit, even if one is valid and the other is off target.

If one fencer should hit on the valid target and the other miss completely, then the valid hit will count.

The action of defending is known as '**parrying**' and hitting back following a successful parry is known as 'riposting'. Fencers will be trained to produce a variety of attacks so that they may 'deceive' their opponent's attempts to parry and riposte.

During a bout, both fencers will be trying to create a moment when they may catch the opponent 'off guard' in order to deliver a successful attack, but they must be continually aware that they may themselves be attacked, and must parry and riposte.

The game, then, becomes a test of concentration, tactical awareness, explosive actions and immediate reactions.

Holding the foil

When the foil is held correctly, it is possible to place the point to the opponent's target with accuracy and sufficient pressure to make the blade bend, but without using excessive force.

With a French handle, place the thumb of your sword hand close to the cushion, lying it flat on the top edge of the foil handle, and curl your index finger around underneath. The last three fingers of the sword hand should

▲ 'French grip'

▲ 'Orthopaedic' or 'pistol' grip

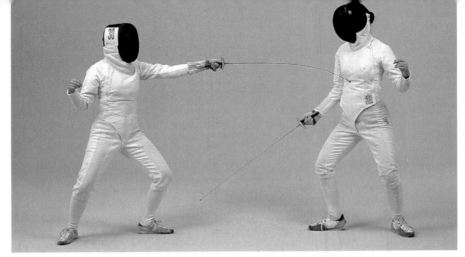

▲ *The hit is made by lowering the point while extending the sword arm. The blade must bend slightly, and the sword hand and shoulder should be relaxed*

rest on the handle, pressing the pommel lightly into the wrist.

When the sword arm is bent at the elbow, a straight line must be formed between the elbow and the point of the foil, the foil forming an extension of the sword arm. The two central fingers of the sword hand should pass through the martingale.

Orthopaedic handles are held in the same way, but with fingers fitting into the mouldings.

Hitting

The correct method of hitting ensures the greatest chance of scoring on the opponent's target; this is not always easy when moving at speed.

Start your practice by hitting a stationary target – a wall pad or a willing partner who is fully kitted – and stand at a distance where you can hit by just extending your sword arm.

Push with your thumb and lower the foil point while extending your arm. Tighten your grip as the blade bends, and hold the hit on the target.

Try to keep your shoulder relaxed all the time, and avoid *punching* the hit.

You should practise hitting at different distances, with a bent arm, with a fully extended arm, or while lunging.

The foil target

The target is the trunk of the body from the top of the neck down to a 'V' at the groin, from the hips at the front and down to a horizontal line across the hip bones at the back and sides.

The arms are not included down from the seams of the sleeves joining the body of the jacket, and neither is the bib of the mask which partly covers the neck and chest.

Guards

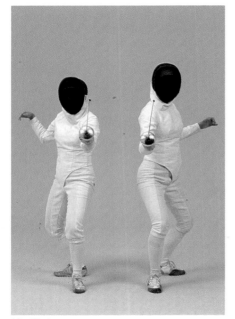

▲ *Sixte*

▲ *Quarte*

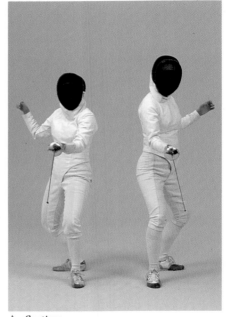

▲ *Septime*

▲ *Octave*

Parries

When defending against the opponent's attack, it is necessary to oppose and deflect the oncoming *foible* with your own *forte*. To enable you to score immediately with a riposte, it is essential that your parry finishes in a correct position.

The direction in which the blade travels determines the name of the parry. (The dotted lines in the following photographs show the initial positions of the sword arm.)

▲ *Simple parry: a lateral movement of the sword arm (in the high line – from sixte to quarte, or vice versa)*

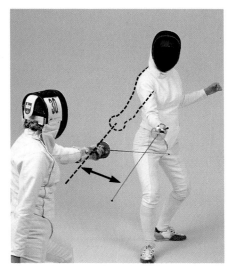

▲ *Simple parry: a lateral movement of the sword arm (in the low line – from octave to septime, or vice versa)*

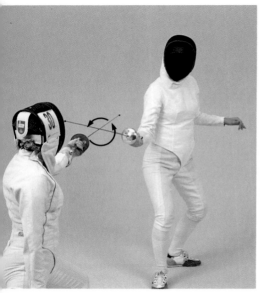

▲ *Circular parry of sixte*

▲ *Circular parry of quarte*

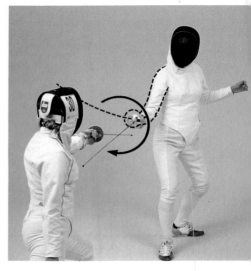

▲ *Semi-circular parry: from sixte to octave, or vice versa*

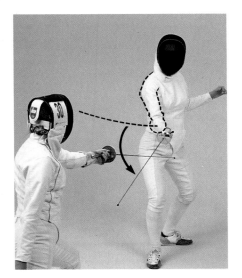

▲ *Semi-circular parry: from quarte to septime, or vice versa*

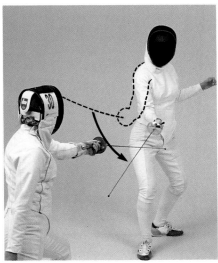

▲ *Diagonal parry: from sixte to septime, or vice versa*

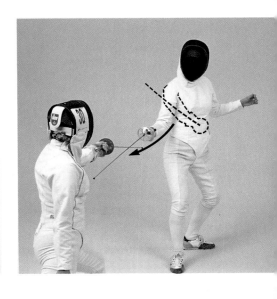

▲ *Diagonal parry: from quarte to octave, or vice versa*

Simple attacks

The object of making an attack is to score a hit on your opponent's valid target.

To do this you have to avoid the opponent's defending blade, which may be moving in a lateral, circular, semi-circular or diagonal direction.

Before making an attack, you must reconnoitre, study the opponent's defence, and make your attack accordingly.

Attacks can be made with a lunge or flèche. Indirect attacks must be made with the minimum of movement, and the foil must be manipulated using the thumb and forefinger of the sword hand.

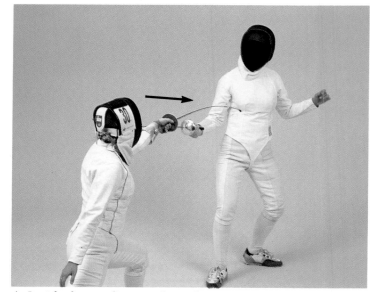

▲ *Straight thrust: a direct attack into the open line (not necessary to pass over or under the opponent's blade)*

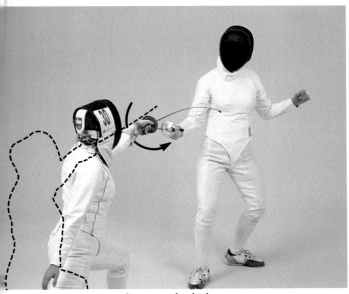

▲ *Disengage: an indirect attack which passes under the opponent's blade*

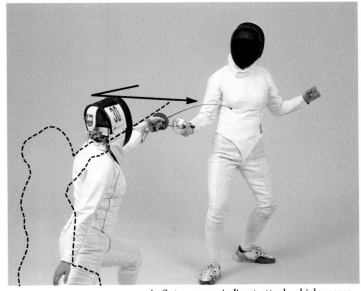

▲ *Cut-over: an indirect attack which passes over the opponent's blade*

Compound attacks

Compound attacks are two or more simple attacks executed in succession.

The first simple attack is made as a 'feint' or false attack to draw the opponent's parry. The subsequent movements of the attack deceive this to deliver the hit.

Simple parries are deceived with one-twos, circular parries with doubles, and semi-circular parries with low-high compound attacks.

Preparations of attack

To create the best conditions in which to make a successful attack during a bout, it may be necessary to start with a preparation.

This may be a fast step forwards or balestra, before the lunge or flèche, to get closer and surprise the opponent, or cause the two foil blades to come into contact – 'engagement' – either with a pressure or by sharply striking the opponent's blade – 'beat'.

A successful preparation can have the effect of making the opponent momentarily 'freeze' or over-react.

Defence on the lunge

Having made an attack with a lunge which has been successfully parried by the opponent, the attacker must defend against the immediate riposte. There will be no time to recover from the lunge, so the parry and 'counter riposte' must be made from the lunge position.

It is essential that fencers develop a powerful lunge which finishes in a stable position. This is impossible with a flèche.

Fencing with the épée

The rules governing foil fencing – termed 'conventions' – do not apply to épée. Because the whole body, including arms, legs and head, is a valid target, the concept of a hit without being hit is fundamental to épée theory, just as it would be in a duel with sharp swords.

Unlike in a duel, épée fencers normally have to score a number of valid hits in a bout to win, but if both hit each other within $\frac{1}{25}$ of a second, then both score a hit.

The épéeist is trained to react to an oncoming attack from the opponent by counter-attacking, usually to the attacking fencer's sword arm, either by 'angulating' the épée to avoid the attack, or by engaging and holding the opponent's blade, 'in opposition', while scoring a hit.

It is also a common technique to use 'renewals', additional attempts to hit, following an initial attack or counter attack.

Many of the actions used at foil are also used by the épéeist, although more care is taken not to expose the sword arm to attacks and counter attacks.

A keen awareness of distance is necessary to avoid being taken by surprise by a direct attack to the body, leg or foot.

▼ *Fencer On Guard with épée*

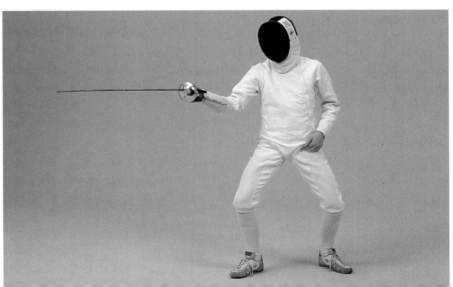

Attacks

Direct attack (to leg) ▶

Attack with opposition (body) ▶

Counter attacks

Counter attack with angulation (arm) ▶

Counter attack with opposition (body) ▶

Fencing with the sabre

The necessity to defend the trunk of the body above the hips, head and arms against hits with both the point and edge cuts at sabre, involves holding the weapon in a different way to that at foil and épée.

The conventions at sabre are the same as those at foil, so it is necessary to parry the opponent's attack before gaining the right to riposte. As defensive movements are large and easily deceived, defence with distance (defending fencer moving back) while trying to access and close the attacker's final line, is a primary tactic.

This is often anticipated by the attacker, who will precede the attack with a running preparation ending with a lunge or flèche.

This, in turn, presents an opportunity for the sabreur who is moving away to attack into the opponent's running preparation either with a cut to the opponent's sword arm, or by maintaining an extended sword arm with the point in line with the oncoming target.

Holding the sabre

Grip ▶

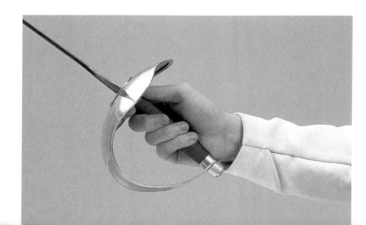

Hitting

◀ *Cut to flank*   ▲ *Cut to head*

▲ *Cut to chest*   ▼ *Point in line*

The target

Guards

▲ *Front view*

▲ *Back view*

▲ *Prime*

▲ *Seconde*

▲ *Tierce*

▲ *Quarte*

35

Fencing on a piste

Organised bouts and matches are conducted on a 'piste' which is 14 m long and 2 m wide.

There are two On Guard lines marked 2 m either side of the centre line. Two further lines are marked 2 m in from either end of the piste, and these sections are shaded. They indicate to the fencers that they are approaching the rear limits.

Either fencer may move forwards or backwards as necessary, but they may not cross the boundaries of the piste, or change ends while fencing.

▲ *Quinte*

Before the bout begins, both fencers must be behind their respective On Guard lines.

The fencers having saluted and put on their masks, the 'president', who referees the fight, gives the instruction to come 'On Guard' and asks if both fencers are 'ready'. If they both are ready, then he says 'Play'.

The bout continues until the president gives the instruction to 'halt'. Both fencers must stop immediately and maintain their positions on the piste until the president has either awarded a hit or restarted the bout.

After each valid hit is awarded, both fencers must resume their positions in the centre of the piste behind their respective On Guard lines.

If either fencer is forced back to a position where both his feet cross the rear limit line, then the president calls 'Halt' and the opponent is awarded a hit. The president also calls 'Halt' when a fencer crosses the side lines with one foot. The fencers are replaced On Guard correctly on the piste, and the bout is restarted. A fencer who crosses a side line with both feet is penalised by having to move backwards 1 m before

▲ *Fencers wired to a box*

the bout is restarted. Fencers cannot score a valid hit when they have both feet off the piste. If there is a simultaneous hit by both fencers, and one fencer is off the piste and the other on, even just with one foot, then only the fencer who is still on the piste will score.

Recreational fencing on a piste and some club matches use judges in addition to a president to watch both fencers and to indicate, by raising their hands, when the fencers have been hit on or off target.

Two judges stand either side of the piste at one end, and both watch the fencer on the opposite end. Two judges are similarly positioned at the opposite end of the piste to watch the other fencer.

The president occupies the area between both sets of judges in such a way that he has a clear view of all four judges and both fencers.

Electrical recording apparatus for registering hits on or off target is used for most competition fencing.

For foil and sabre, each fencer wears a metallic lamé jacket which covers just the target area. They use special weapons which are wired to a recording box through a spool with a retractable lead.

When a hit is made on target, a coloured light shows on the recording box and a buzzer sounds. A red light shows for one fencer, a green light for his opponent.

At foil, white lights indicate off-target hits.

Metallic jackets are not necessary for épée because the whole body is a valid target.

The president controls and referees the bout, using the lights on the recording box to determine valid hits.

Training

Fencing cannot be learned thoroughly unless you start by joining a class at a local club. The coach will be able to explain fully and demonstrate all the elementary skills. You will be able to practise these with your class colleagues, and see how they fit into the overall game.

Specific group footwork training will develop mobility, and individual lessons with the coach will improve technical skills and tactical knowledge.

Competitive training in the form of 'theme' fencing exercises and training competitions are useful for monitoring improvement.

Coaches will also advise on physical preparation, warm-up and stretching. Regular fencing training will develop overall endurance, flexibility and co-ordination.

Fencers who compete on a regular basis will learn how to plan their training to fit in with their competition programme, and to set primary and intermediate 'goals'.

Tactics

In competitive fencing the choice of the right stroke must be combined with the ability to execute it not only correctly, but at the right time and distance. Co-ordination of mind and body is one of the major factors; this is brought about by confidence in one's technical ability to execute any action that might be required. This confidence will help relieve stress and allow you to relax and achieve the required co-ordination.

The form of attack is generally dictated by your opponent's defensive actions. If his defensive movements are of a circular nature, then your attacks must also be circular in order to deceive and hit. Most fencers have favourite strokes or actions, and these are discovered by watching your opponent's response or feeling those movements through your blade (*sentiment du fer*). This tactical approach may be applied in the early stages of the bout by reconnaissance actions, feints, simple attacks, false attacks, etc.

A conscious effort must be made to vary your own game because your opponent will, of course, be trying to anticipate your next movement by noting your habits. You can counter-bluff by reacting to his exploratory moves in a way to induce him to use a particular stroke, which you may turn to your own advantage.

Attacks and ripostes, however well chosen, will often fail unless they are delivered at the right moment and at the right speed. For example, a disengage should be timed as the opponent's blade is moving away from the line in which you intend to hit him, not while it is moving to close that line. Similarly, it is an advantage to launch an attack at the moment your opponent is himself preparing to attack and is therefore momentarily less vigilant in defence. It is equally important to adjust the speed of a stroke to that of the opponent's timing and rhythm. For example, a 'one-two' may fail because it is made so fast that the slower reacting opponent will not respond to the feint, therefore his blade will not have moved away from the original line of engagement.

The opponent's speed or cadence is ascertained during the initial exploratory moves mentioned above. It is often possible to impose one's own cadence during a bout by varying the cadence of one's own movements. At this point a sudden speeding up of the final movement or a broken time attack may achieve success.

A sense of distance must be developed by practice. Changes of distance by stepping forwards or back can be used tactically to make it more difficult for the opponent to time his attacks or preparations. The boxing adage 'Box a fighter, fight a boxer' applies just as well at fencing. Attack an attacker but not the fencer who relies on his defence to score hits. Confuse the stop-hitter so that he either misses or hits out of time. When fencing an opponent with a long reach who continually renews his attack, shorten the distance by stepping forwards into his attack to give him less room to manoeuvre, so disrupting his precision.

Against the fencer who will not give the blade, false attacks or well marked feints can be used to draw his reaction. If this is a stop hit, meet it with a counter-time, preferably taking the blade. If he makes a parry, a composed attack or a counter-riposte may score or if he returns to engagement, an appropriate attack can be made.

When fencing an opponent who habitually attacks into the attack, draw his attack prematurely by a false attack with a half lunge or by a change of measure to score with attacks on the blade or ripostes.

Fencing at close quarters is often effective at foil provided one has sufficient blade control; it is less safe at épée and sabre. At close quarters at épée it is best immediately to force the *corps-à-corps*, taking care to do so without violence or to avoid being hit. (These last two are offences, subject to penalty under the rules.)

The flèche attack is especially effective at épée and sabre, and as a riposte against an opponent who makes a rapid recovery after being parried, or to conclude a second intention attack.

Against an opponent who is faster than oneself, it is often possible to disconcert him and regain the initiative by making changes of engagement in varying tempo.

If difficulty is found in analysing an opponent's game, it is best to increase the distance, thus obtaining more time to study his methods by forcing him to make longer preparations of his attacks.

Use the piste tactically. Do not waste ground by retiring unnecessarily and take every opportunity to regain ground lost during a bout. On the other hand, forcing a defensive fencer back on to his rear line may induce him to attack or, if one is superior in defence, the opponent may be induced to attack by retiring to one's own rear line.

Left-handers are often vulnerable to attacks or ripostes which end in the low lines, particularly at flank. Feints into octave sometimes induce left-handers to leave the quarte or high lines open to attack.

Glossary

Absence of blade: when swords are not in contact.

Advance: to step forwards.

Aids: the last three fingers of the sword hand.

Analysis: the process of describing actions occurring in a fight, usually a phrase preceding a hit.

Angulation: creating an angle between the weapon and the sword arm by flexing the wrist and pronating or supinating the sword hand.

Annulment of hit: a valid hit which is disallowed because of an infringement of the rules or a technical fault.

Appel: beating the ground with the ball of the foot, either as a 'front foot' or 'rear foot' appel.

Arrêt: *see* stop hit.

Assault: friendly combat between two fencers.

Attack: an initial offensive action made by extending the sword arm and continuously threatening the opponent's target.

Avoidance: ducking or moving sideways to avoid being hit.

Back edge: the edge of a sabre blade opposite to that of the cutting edge.

Balestra: a short, sharp jump forwards; usually used as a preparation.

Barrage: a fight-off to determine a result in the event of a tie.

Beat: crisp striking movement of the opponent's blade creating a deflection, or obtaining a reaction; used as a preparation.

Bib: a soft, padded attachment to the lower part of the mask to protect the neck and throat.

Bind: taking of the foible of the opposing blade diagonally from high to low line, and vice versa.

Blade: the main component of a sword on which the hilt is mounted.

Body wire: wire worn under a fencer's

clothing to connect the sword terminal to the retractable spool cable, when using the electrical apparatus.

Bout: a fight for a specific number of hits.

Breaking ground: stepping back.

Breeches: white, knee-length trousers made of robust material; side fastening must be on the non-sword-arm side, and legs must have fastenings below the knees.

Broken time: when a pause is introduced into an action which is normally performed in one movement.

Brutality: actions which are performed with an unacceptable level of force or violence which causes discomfort to the opponent.

Button: soft covering over a non-electric foil or épée point.

Cadence: the rhythm in which a sequence of movements is made.

Ceding parry: a parry formed by giving way to an opponent who is taking the blade.

Change beat: a beat made after passing under or over the opponent's blade.

Change of engagement: re-engagement of the opponent's blade on the opposite side by passing under or over it.

Chest protectors: rigid breast cups which fit inside women's fencing jackets.

Choice reaction: reasoned response to a change of conditions presented by the opponent.

Circular parry: deflection of the opponent's attacking blade by making a circle with the sword point.

Close quarters: when two fencers are close together but can still wield their weapons.

Competition: aggregate of individual bouts or team matches required to determine a winner.

Compound actions: two or more single actions performed together as one continuous action.

Compound attack: an attack comprising one or more feints.

Compound prises de fer: two or more consecutive takings of the blade, alike or different, with no loss of blade contact.

Compound riposte: riposte comprising one or more feints.

Conventions: the rules governing the method of fencing for each weapon.

Coquille: bell-shaped guard of a foil or épée.

Corps à corps: bodily contact between the fencers in a bout.

Coulé: the action of extending the sword arm and grazing lightly down the opponent's blade, maintaining contact throughout.

Counter attack: the offensive action made while avoiding, or closing the line against, an opponent's attack.

Counter-disengagement: an indirect action which deceives a change of engagement.

Counter-offensive action: *see* counter attack.

Counter-parry: *see* circular parry.

Counter-riposte: a riposte following the successful parry of the opponent's riposte or counter-riposte.

Counter-time: an action made by the attacker into a counter attack which is provoked by the opponent.

Coupé: *see* cut-over.

Croisé: the taking of the foible of the opposing blade from high to low line, and vice versa, on the same side as the engagement.

Crosse grip: a moulded grip with finger protrusions, used on foils and épées.

Cut: a hit at sabre made by striking with the edge of the blade.

Cut-over (coupé): an indirect action made by passing the blade over the opponent's point.

Defence: not being hit by the opponent's offensive actions, either by parrying, avoiding, or moving out of distance.

Delayed: actions made after a pause; usually attacks or ripostes.

Dérobement: evasion of the opponent's

attempt to beat or take the blade while the sword arm is straight and the point is threatening the target.

Detachment: when both blades break contact.

Development: extension of the sword arm accompanied by the lunge.

Diagonal parry: deflecting the opponent's attacking blade by moving from a high line guard to a low line guard on the opposite side, and vice versa.

Direct: actions made without passing the blade under or over the opponent's blade.

Direct elimination: method of competition organisation where winners are promoted to the following rounds and losers are eliminated after one fight.

Disciplinary code: by taking part in a fencing competition, fencers 'pledge their honour' to observe the rules for competitions and the decisions of judges, and to be respectful towards the president and the members of the jury.

Disengagement: indirect action made by passing the blade under or over the opponent's blade.

Displacement: turning or ducking to remove the target area from its normal position, resulting in the non-valid target being substituted for the valid target.

Disqualification: to be eliminated from a competition due to cheating or bad behaviour, or by default, e.g. late arrival.

Doublé: a compound attack which deceives the opponent's circular parry.

Double action: when both fencers choose exactly the same moment to make an offensive action.

Double defeat: in épée only; after the time has expired, if both competitors have received the same number of hits (or neither has scored a hit), they are counted as both having received the maximum number of hits being fought for, and a defeat is scored against each, except in direct elimination where the fight goes on without limitation of time until there is a result.

Double hits: in épée only, when both competitors register a hit on each other simultaneously, the difference of time between the two hits being less than $\frac{1}{25}$ of a second.

Double prises de fer: loss of contact between the first and second prise de fer.

Draw: seeding of fencers to determine the bouts in a competition.

Duration of bout: actual fencing time allowed during a bout, i.e. a stop clock is started at the beginning of a bout, stopped each time the president halts the fencers, and started again when the bout is restarted.

Earthing of guard: guards of electric weapons must be earthed correctly so that weapon hits do not register on them.

Earthing of piste: when using electrical equipment, metal pistes must be correctly earthed so that hits do not register on them.

Elbow guard: a pad worn on the fencer's sword-arm elbow for protection.

Electrical apparatus: an electric box with red and green lights to register valid hits at foil, épée and sabre, and white lights to register non-valid hits at foil. The apparatus is mounted centrally, adjacent to the piste, and connected by floor leads to spools with retractable cables placed at both ends of the piste, to which the fencers connect their body wires.

Electric weapons: foils, épées and sabres suitable for use with electrical apparatus.

Engagement: when both blades are in contact.

Envelopment: the taking of the foible of the opponent's blade by making a complete circle and maintaining continual contact throughout.

Epée: modern version of the duelling rapier, with a triangular section blade and a bell-shaped guard; valid hits are made with the point on any part of the opponent's body.

False actions: actions made to assess the opponent's reaction or to provoke a reaction which can be exploited.

Feint: threatening movement of the blade made with the intention of provoking a parry or similar response.

Fencing line: when fencers are fencing each other it should be possible to draw a theoretical straight line running through both leading feet and rear heels.

Fencing measure: the distance between two fencers such that they must lunge fully to score a valid hit.

Fencing position: the position adopted by a fencer to maintain a guard.

Fencing time: the time required to perform one simple fencing action.

FIE: Fédération Internationale d'Escrime – the international governing body of fencing.

Finger play: a method of manipulating a weapon with the fingers.

Flank: the side of the trunk of body on the sword-arm side.

Flèche (arrow): offensive movement made by leaning forwards so as to cause a loss of balance.

Floor judges: two judges who watch for floor hits when electric épée is used without a metal piste.

Foible: the flexible half of the blade further away from the hilt.

Foil (fleuret): originally developed as a practice version of the small sword, the foil has a rectangular section and a flexible blade with a protected point. Valid hits are scored by hitting with the point on the opponent's trunk. Hits on the arms, legs and head do not count as valid hits.

Forte: the half of the blade nearer to the hilt.

French grip: the hilt style which has a straight handle (without finger protrusions) and a pommel.

Froissement: deflecting the opponent's blade by opposition of 'forte to foible' while blades are engaged.

Gaining ground: stepping forwards.

Glove: made of leather or similar material which must be worn on the sword hand and which must have a gauntlet long enough to cover the sword arm sleeve mid-way between the hand and the elbow.

Graze: *see* coulé.

Grip (of weapon): the handle part of the hilt.

Grip: the method of holding the sword.

Guard (of weapon): the part of the hilt to protect the sword hand.

Guards: fencing positions – *see* prime, seconde, tierce, quarte, quinte, sixte, septime, octave.

High line: the position of the target above a theoretical horizontal line mid-way through a fencer's trunk.

Hilt: the assembled parts of the sword excluding the blade, i.e. the guard, pad, grip and pommel.

Hit: to strike the opponent with the point of the sword clearly and distinctly and with character of penetration. A cut with a sabre.

Immediate: an action made without a pause.

Indicators: a system used in competition to determine a fencer's seeding after the first rounds. The first indicator is expressed as a ratio of the number of victories and the number of fights, and the second indicator is the number of hits scored minus the number of hits received.

Indirect: an offensive action made by first passing the blade under or over the opponent's blade.

Italian foil/épée: weapons which have hilts with guards and cross bars.

Jacket: a jacket made of white, robust material without fastenings on the sword-arm side, which covers the valid target and has double thickness material on the front and on the sword arm.

Judges: in non-electric bouts, four judges officiate, two at both sides of the piste, to watch for hits on the fencer they are facing. Judges may also officiate during bouts using electric equipment to watch for illegal use of back arm, or hits on the floor when metallic pistes are not used.

Jury: the president and judges who officiate during a bout.

Jury d'appel: at a competition, a fencer or team captain may ask for a jury d'appel to be convened if he believes a misapplication of the rules has occurred. The jury will consist of one representative of each competing nation, or members of the organising committee.

Lamé jacket: metallic-woven over-jacket covering the valid target for foil and for sabre.

Lines: theoretical divisions of the target, corresponding to fencing guards.

Low lines: position of the target below a theoretical horizontal line mid-way through a fencer's trunk.

Lunge: a method of getting closer to an opponent with acceleration to make an attack, and while maintaining balance and making it possible for a rapid recovery to On Guard.

Manipulators: the index finger and thumb of the sword hand.

Martingale: the loop of tape or leather attached to the grip and held to prevent a non-electric foil from flying out of the hand in the event of being disarmed.

Mask: wire mesh covering worn on the head to protect the face, sides of the head and neck.

Metallic piste: electrically-conductive material covering the piste in order that hits on the floor do not register on the electrical apparatus.

Octave: low line, semi-supinated guard on the sword-arm side.

On Guard: the stance adopted in fencing.

One-two attack: a compound attack which deceives the opponent's simple parry.

'Open eyes': starting a movement with no prior knowledge of how it will finish, relying on reflexes to adjust and make the correct ending.

Opposition: blade movement maintaining constant contact with the opponent's blade.

Orthopaedic grip: general term for moulded grips of various designs used on foils and épées.

Parry: defensive action to deflect an opponent's attack by opposing 'forte to opponent's foible'.

Part-whole: the teaching of a movement in 'parts', i.e. isolating the 'parts' of the movement demanding most skill and practising them in isolation; then putting the 'parts' together to make a 'whole' movement.

Patinando: a step forwards with an appel from the rear foot at the same time as the front foot lands.

Phrase: a sequence of fencing movements performed without a break.

Piste: the field of play on which a bout takes place.

Plastron: a half-jacket with no under-arm seam, worn for extra protection on the sword arm under the fencing jacket; also a padded over-jacket worn by a fencing coach when giving individual training.

Pommel: a metal cap screwed to the end of the blade which locks the parts of the weapon together and provides a counter-balance to the blade.

Pool (poule): the grouping of fencers or teams in a competition.

Preparation of attack: the movement of blade or foot to obtain the best position from which to make an attack.

President: the referee in a fencing bout.

Pressure: the pressing movement of the fencer's blade against the opponent's blade, to deflect it or to cause a reaction from it.

Prime: high line, pronated guard on the non-sword-arm side.

Principle of defence: the execution of a parry by the defender's forte opposing the attacking foible, i.e. 'opposition of forte to foible'.

Priority: the right of way gained by the fencer at foil and sabre by extending the sword arm and continually threatening the opponent's target.

Prises de fer (takings of the blade): *see* bind, croisé, envelopment.

Progressive actions: actions made with the sword point continually moving towards the opponent's target.

Pronation: the position of the sword hand with the knuckles uppermost.

Quarte: high line, semi-supinated guard on the non-sword-arm side.

Quinte: low line, pronated guard on the non-sword-arm side at foil and épée; and a high guard at sabre to protect the head.

Rassemblement: the bringing of both feet together, either forwards or backwards, so that the heels are touching with the feet at right angles and the body in an upright position.

Reaction: a response to a stimulus; a reflex or a controlled reflex action.

Recovery: the return to the On Guard position.

Redoublement: the renewal of an action after being parried by replacing the point on the target in a different line to the original action.

Remise: the renewal of an action after being parried by replacing the point on the target in the line of the original action.

Renewals of attack: *see* remise, redoublement, reprise.

Renewed actions: the continuation of the original offensive action following the opponent's parry.

Repechage: the competition formula which gives losers of a direct elimination bout a second chance to stay in the competition.

Reprise: the renewal of an action made with a lunge by first returning to guard forwards or backwards.

Retire: to step back.

Riposte: an offensive action following a successful parry of an attack.

Sabre: a light, flexible version of the military sabre. Hits can be scored by using edge 'cuts' or point thrusts; only hits scored on the opponent's body above the waist, arms and head count as valid.

Salute: the acknowledgement of respect shown to an opponent, fencing coach or training partner before crossing swords.

Seconde: low line, pronated guard on the sword-arm side.

Second-intention: an action made to provoke a movement from the opponent.

Semi-circular parry: the deflection of the attacking blade by making a semicircle with the point of the sword, from high to low line on the same side, and vice versa.

Sentiment du fer: the use of the tactile senses of the fingers ('feel of the blade'), mainly thumb and forefinger, to give an awareness of the blade.

Septime: low line, semi-supinated guard on the non-sword-arm side.

Simple attack: an offensive action made with one blade movement in one period of fencing time; may be direct or indirect.

Simple parry: the deflection of the attacking blade by application of 'forte to foible', the sword arm moving horizontally across the body from sixte to quarte, and vice versa, and from octave to septime, and vice versa.

Simultaneous attack: when both fencers choose precisely the same moment to make an offensive action.

Sixte: high line, semi-supinated guard on the sword-arm side.

Spools: part of the electrical apparatus which has retractable cables to connect the fencers to the electrical recording box.

Stance: the position of the feet and legs of the fencer while in the On Guard position.

Stop cut/stop point: counter-offensive action at sabre.

Stop hit (arrêt): counter-offensive action into the opponent's attack.

Stop hit in opposition: counter-offensive action which closes the line against the opponent's attack.

Straight thrust: a direct attack landing in the same line.

Successive parries: two or more consecutive parries made to defend against compound attacks.

Supination: the position of the sword hand with the finger-nail uppermost.

Takings of the blade (prises de fer): *see* bind, croisé, envelopment.

Tang: the part of the blade on which the hilt is mounted.

Target (épée): the whole of the body including the back, hands, feet and head.

Target (foil): the trunk of the body, excluding the head and limbs. The upper limit is the collar up to 6 cm above the prominences of the collar bones; at the sides to the seams which should cross the head of the humerus. The lower limit follows a horizontal line across the back joining the tops of the hip bones, thence following in straight lines to the junction of the lines of the groin. (Note: the bib of the mask is 'off target'.)

Target (sabre): any part of the body above a horizontal line drawn between the top of the folds formed by the thighs and by the trunk of the fencer when in the On Guard position.

Temps d'escrime: *see* fencing time.

Tierce: high line, pronated guard on the sword-arm side.

Trompement: the deception of the opponent's attempt to parry.

Valid hit: a hit which arrives correctly on target.

Index